Celebrate with Me
Celebra conmigo

CHRISTMAS
NAVIDAD

Mitchell Lane

PUBLISHERS

P.O. Box 196
Hockessin, Delaware 19707
Visit us on the web: www.mitchelllane.com
Comments? email us:
mitchelllane@mitchelllane.com

Mitchell Lane
PUBLISHERS

Printing   1   2   3   4   5   6   7   8   9

A LITTLE JAMIE BOOK

Celebrate with Me

Christmas
Independence Day
Memorial Day
Thanksgiving

Celebra conmigo

Navidad
Día de la Independencia
Día de los Caídos
Acción de Gracias

Library of Congress Cataloging-in-Publication Data applied for.

ABOUT THE AUTHOR: Bonnie Hinman has written over twenty books for young people, including *Threat to the Leatherback Turtle* and *Celebrate with Me: Thanksgiving* for Mitchell Lane Publishers. Bonnie loves celebrating Christmas with her four grandchildren. She makes sure there is always plenty of loot under the tree.

ACERCA DE LA AUTORA: Bonnie Hinman ha escrito más de veinte libros para jóvenes, que incluyen *Threat to the Leatherback Turtle* and *Celebra conmigo: Acción de Gracias* para Mitchell Lane Publishers. A Bonnie le encanta celebrar la Navidad con sus cuatro nietos. Se asegura de que siempre haya muchos regalos debajo del árbol.

ABOUT THE TRANSLATOR: Eida de la Vega was born in Havana, Cuba, and now lives in New Jersey with her mother, her husband, and her two children. Eida has worked at Lectorum/Scholastic, and as editor of the magazine *Selecciones del Reader's Digest*.

ACERCA DE LA TRADUCTORA: Eida de la Vega nació en La Habana, Cuba, y ahora vive en Nueva Jersey con su madre, su esposo y sus dos hijos. Ha trabajado en Lectorum/Scholastic y, como editora, en la revista *Selecciones del Reader's Digest*.

Celebrate with Me
Celebra conmigo

CHRISTMAS
NAVIDAD

BY/POR
BONNIE HINMAN

TRANSLATED BY/
TRADUCIDO POR
EIDA DE LA VEGA

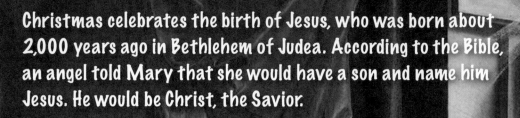

Christmas celebrates the birth of Jesus, who was born about 2,000 years ago in Bethlehem of Judea. According to the Bible, an angel told Mary that she would have a son and name him Jesus. He would be Christ, the Savior.

La Navidad celebra el nacimiento de Jesús, que ocurrió hace más de 2000 años en Belén de Judea. De acuerdo con la Biblia, un ángel le dijo a María que tendría un hijo que se llamaría Jesús. Sería Cristo, el Salvador.

Mary and her husband, Joseph, traveled from their home in Nazareth to Bethlehem. The inns were full, so Mary and Joseph had to stay in a stable. Jesus was born there and laid in a manger. His birth is called the Nativity.

María y su esposo, José, viajaron desde su casa en Nazaret hasta Belén. Las posadas estaban tan llenas que María y José tuvieron que quedarse en un establo. Allí, en un pesebre, nació Jesús. Su nacimiento se llama la Natividad.

Three Wise Men from the east were guided to Bethlehem by a star. They rode many miles on their camels to bring gifts to the infant Jesus. Shepherds also followed the star to Bethlehem.

Tres Reyes Magos del Oriente fueron guiados por una estrella a Belén. Cabalgaron muchas millas en camellos para llevarle regalos al Niño Jesús. También muchos pastores siguieron la estrella hasta Belén.

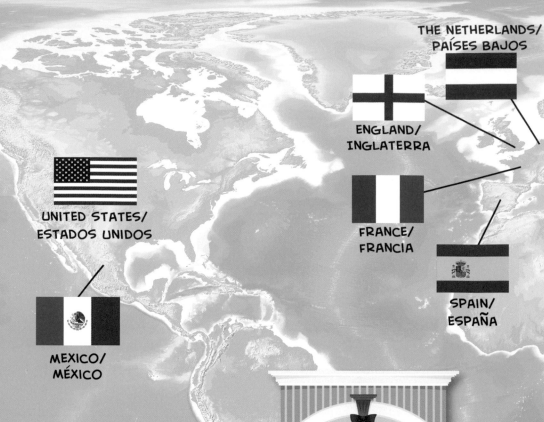

THE NETHERLANDS/
PAÍSES BAJOS

ENGLAND/
INGLATERRA

UNITED STATES/
ESTADOS UNIDOS

FRANCE/
FRANCIA

SPAIN/
ESPAÑA

MEXICO/
MÉXICO

Merry
Christmas!

Christians around the world celebrate Christmas. Not all of
their customs are the same, but many are. The symbols of
Christmas—the Nativity, the star, the shepherd's crook, and
the spirit of giving—can be found in many countries. Drums
are common, too. They represent the humble drummer boy
who played his drum as a gift for the Christ Child.

8

GERMANY/
ALEMANIA

BETHLEHEM/
BELÉN

CHINA

INDIA

AUSTRALIA

¡FELIZ NAVIDAD!

En todo el mundo, los cristianos celebran la Navidad. Muchas de las tradiciones, aunque no todas, son iguales. Los símbolos de la Navidad —la Natividad, la estrella, el cayado de pastor y el espíritu de regalar— pueden encontrarse en muchos países. Los tambores también son comunes. Representan al humilde niño pastor que tocó su tambor como un regalo para el Niño Jesús.

In France, Christmas begins on December 6 with St. Nicholas Day. Children leave their shoes or stockings near the fireplace, and Père Noël fills them with nuts, fruit, and small toys. After church at midnight on Christmas Eve, the French enjoy a huge meal with a special dessert called *la bûche de Noël*, or chocolate yule log.

En Francia, la Navidad empieza el 6 de diciembre, el día de San Nicolás. Los niños dejan los zapatos o las medias cerca de la chimenea, y Père Noël las llena con nueces, frutas y juguetes pequeños. En Nochebuena, después de ir a la iglesia a medianoche, los franceses disfrutan de un postre especial llamado la bûche de Noël, o tronco de Navidad de chocolate.

In The Netherlands, Sinterklass arrives by ship from Spain, then rides a white horse through town. On St. Nicholas Day Eve, December 5, children leave their shoes out for Sinterklass to fill with gifts. People serve *kerstkrans*, which is a Christmas ring pastry.

En los Países Bajos, Sinterklass llega en barco desde España, y se pasea por la ciudad montado en un caballo blanco. La víspera de San Nicolás, el 5 de diciembre, los niños dejan sus zapatos fuera para que Sinterklass los llene de regalos. Acostumbra servirse kerstkrans, que es una rosca de Navidad.

Christmas religious services in Mexico often end with parties for the children. The children swing a stick at a piñata until it breaks and showers them with candy. Tamales are a traditional Christmas Eve dinner. Red and white poinsettias are originally from Mexico, where they are called Christmas Eve flowers.

Los servicios religiosos navideños en México terminan con frecuencia con fiestas para los niños. Los niños tratan de pegarle con un palo a una piñata hasta que se rompe y cae una lluvia de caramelos. Los tamales son una cena tradicional de Nochebuena. Las poinsettias rojas y blancas son originarias de México, donde se llaman flores de Nochebuena.

It's summer in Australia when Christmas arrives. Sometimes Santa rides onto the beach on a surfboard. After Christmas dinner, Australians have pavlova, a meringue dessert topped with fruit.

Es verano en Australia cuando llega la Navidad. A veces, Santa se pasea por la playa en una tabla de surf. Después de la cena de Navidad, los australianos comen pavlova, un postre de merengue con fruta encima.

In Spain, dinner is served after midnight on Christmas Eve, with flan (baked custard) for dessert. Children in Catalonia, a region of Spain, have fun with Tio de Nadal, the Christmas log. The hollow log is decorated to look like Santa. It hides candy, nuts, and sometimes presents. The Three Wise Men bring gifts to children on Epiphany, January 6.

En España, la cena se sirve después de medianoche, el día de Nochebuena, con flan de postre. Los niños en Cataluña, una región de España, se divierten con el Tío de Nadal, un tronco de Navidad. El tronco hueco se decora de modo que se parezca a Santa. Dentro se esconden caramelos, nueces y, a veces, regalos. Los tres Reyes Magos les traen regalos a los niños el día de la Epifanía, el 6 de enero.

Christians in China celebrate Christmas with bright lights on buildings and trees, fireworks, and church services. Children hang their stockings on Christmas Eve, hoping Dun Che Lao Ren, China's version of Santa Claus, will fill them with gifts. Peking duck is a popular main dish for Christmas dinner.

Dun Che Lao Ren

China

Christmas in China is called Sheng Dan Jieh, which means the "Holy Birth Festival." The Chinese celebrate Christmas by lighting their homes with beautiful paper lanterns and decorating Christmas trees, which they call "trees of light," with bright, colorful ornaments. These ornaments are made from paper in the shapes of flowers, chains and lanterns.

On Christmas Eve, children hang muslin stockings in hopes that Dun Che Lao Ren or "Christmas Old Man" will fill them with gifts and treats from the wicker basket he carries. Christmas Day is celebrated with a marvelous display of fireworks. Gifts may be exchanged with expensive gifts for the family, and food or flowers for other relatives and friends.

Los cristianos en China celebran la Navidad con luces brillantes en edificios y árboles, fuegos artificiales y servicios religiosos. Los niños cuelgan sus medias en Nochebuena, a la espera de que Dun Che Lao Ren, la versión china de Santa Claus, las llene de regalos. El pato pequinés es un plato muy popular en la cena de Navidad.

It's warm in India at Christmastime, and a Santa sand sculpture celebrates the season. Many families display Nativity scenes. They enjoy *jilebi*, a treat of fried dough soaked in syrup.

En la India, hay calor en la época de Navidad, y una escultura de Santa hecha con arena celebra la temporada. Muchas familias montan escenas de la Natividad. Saborean el jilebi, un dulce que consiste en una masa frita empapada en sirope.

In England, some children parade with paper lanterns, while others gather for caroling. Father Christmas fills stockings with candy and toys on Christmas Eve. Before Christmas dinner, children pull Christmas crackers. These cardboard tubes, which contain small gifts, make a loud crack when pulled apart. After a turkey or goose dinner, dessert is figgy pudding.

En Inglaterra, algunos niños desfilan con linternas de papel, mientras que otros se reúnen para cantar villancicos. En Nochebuena, Papá Navidad (Santa Claus) pone caramelos y juguetes en las medias. Antes de la cena de Navidad, los niños tiran de los extremos de un petardo de Navidad. Estos tubos de cartón, que contienen pequeños regalos, al romperse, provocan una pequeña explosión. Después de una cena de pavo o ganso, el postre es pudín de higos.

In Germany, special Christmas markets sell advent calendars, handcrafted decorations, and snacks such as *stollen*—sweet bread filled with nuts and candied fruit. Christkindl, who represents the spirit of the Christ Child, passes out presents at parties.

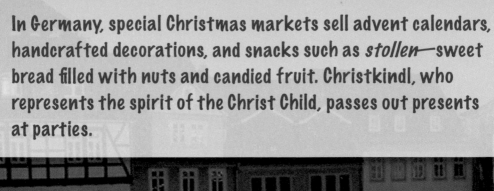

En Alemania, en los mercados navideños, se venden calendarios de adviento, adornos hechos a mano y golosinas como el *stollen*, que consiste en un pan dulce relleno con nueces y frutas confitadas. Christkindl, quien representa el espíritu del Niño Jesús, reparte regalos en fiestas.

Christkindl

28

Many people in the United States start their Christmas preparations on the day after Thanksgiving, when they go gift shopping. Families put up Christmas trees and decorate them with shiny ornaments. Children visit Santa to tell him their Christmas wishes.

Muchas personas en Estados Unidos empiezan sus preparativos navideños el día después de Acción de Gracias, cuando van a comprar regalos. Las familias ponen árboles de Navidad y los decoran con adornos brillantes. Los niños visitan a Santa para contarle sus deseos de Navidad.

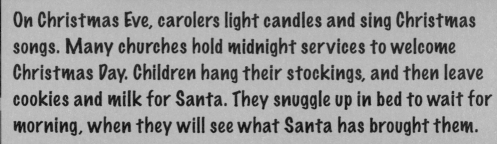

On Christmas Eve, carolers light candles and sing Christmas songs. Many churches hold midnight services to welcome Christmas Day. Children hang their stockings, and then leave cookies and milk for Santa. They snuggle up in bed to wait for morning, when they will see what Santa has brought them.

En Nochebuena, se prenden velas y se cantan villancicos. Muchas iglesias tienen un servicio a medianoche para dar la bienvenida a la Navidad. Los niños cuelgan medias y le dejan galletas y leche a Santa. Se acurrucan en la cama hasta la mañana siguiente, cuando verán lo que les ha traído Santa.

FURTHER READING/LECTURAS RECOMENDADAS

Books for Young Readers

Baum, L. Frank, and Charles Santore (illustrator). *The Life and Adventures of Santa Claus.* Philadelphia: Running Kids Press, 2009.

Flanagan, Alice, and Viki Woodworth (illustrator). *Christmas.* Minneapolis, Minn.: Compass Point Books, 2002.

Tillman, Nancy. *The Spirit of Christmas.* New York: Feiwel & Friends, 2009.

En español

Ada, Alma Flor/ Campoy, Isabel. *Celebra la Navidad y el Día de los Reyes Magos con Pablo y Carlitos (Historias para celebrar).* Alfaguara Infantil, Santillana USA, 2006.

Works Consulted

Charlton, Jim, and Maria Robbins. *A Christmas Companion: Recipes, Traditions, and Customs From Around the World.* New York: Perigee Books, 1989.

Fowler, Virginia. *Christmas Crafts and Customs Around the World.* Englewood Cliffs, New Jersey: Prentice-Hall, 1984.

Gulevich, Tanya, editor. *Encyclopedia of Christmas.* Detroit: Omnigraphics, 2000.

Jeffery, Yvonne. *The Everything Family Christmas Book.* Avon, Massachusetts: Adams Media, 2008.

Snyder, Phillip. *December 25th: The Joys of Christmas Past.* New York: Dodd, Mead & Company, 1985.

Video

Guss, Alison, Clement Moore, and Robert May. *Christmas Unwrapped: The History of Christmas.* A&E Home Video, 1997.

On the Internet

Christmas in Australia
  http://www.the-north-pole.com/around/australia.html
Christmas Traditions
  http://www.merry-christmas.com/traditions.htm
Christmas Traditions in England
  http://www.lovelychristmas.co.uk/EnglishChristmasTraditions.html
The History of Christmas
  http://thehistoryofchristmas.com
Why Christmas?
  http://www.whychristmas.com

En Internet

La Navidad de El Almanaque
  http://www.elalmanaque.com/navidad/mundo.htm
La Navidad Latina
  http://www.navidadlatina.com

INDEX/ÍNDICE